I Hope They Call Me on a
MISSION

Written by Benjamin Hyrum White

Illustrated by Corey Egbert

CFI
An Imprint of Cedar Fort, Inc.
Springville, Utah

ISBN 13: 978-1-4621-1551-8

Published by CFI, an imprint of Cedar Fort, Inc.
2373 W. 700 S., Springville, UT 84663
Distributed by Cedar Fort, Inc., www.cedarfort.com

LIBRARY OF CONGRESS CATALOGING-IN-PUBLICATION DATA

White, Benjamin Hyrum, 1978- author.
I hope they call me on a mission / written by Benjamin Hyrum White ; Illustrated by Corey Egbert.
    pages cm
ISBN 978-1-4621-1551-8 (alk. paper)
1. Mormon missionaries. I. Egbert, Corey, 1988- illustrator. II. Title.

BX8661.W35 2015
266'.93023--dc23

2014036877

Cover design and interior layout design by Shawnda T. Craig
Cover design © 2015 Lyle Mortimer
Edited by Kevin Haws

Printed in China

10 9 8 7 6 5 4 3 2 1

Printed on acid-free paper

"Kids! We got a letter from Uncle Clay on his mission. Let's read it together."

"I hope they call me on a mission!"

"Me too! But . . . what is it like to be a missionary? Let's write Uncle Clay and find out!"

Dear David and Megan, Being a missionary is incredible. Let me tell you about it.

Missionaries EXERCISE

Missionaries need to take care of their physical bodies. Every morning, we exercise. We can walk, jog, or run. We can play basketball, soccer, or any activity approved by our leaders. We also ride bikes.

WHAT CAN YOU DO NOW?

Find physical activities you love that will help you stay active. A healthy body is important for a healthy spirit.

Missionaries have a COMPANION

Missionaries always have someone with them wherever they go. This person is called a companion. Missionaries will have many different companions. These companions often become great friends.

WHAT CAN YOU DO NOW?

Work hard to get along with your parents and siblings. Try to be a good friend to everyone.

Missionaries STUDY and PRAY

Missionaries need divine help every day. We study the scriptures and pray, both on our own and with our missionary companion. We love to pray and read the scriptures with the families we visit.

WHAT CAN YOU DO NOW?

Create good habits of gospel study and prayer. Search the scriptures, read the Church magazines, and discuss them with your family. Make morning and evening prayers a priority. Get your own copy of *Preach My Gospel.*

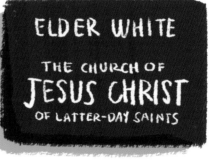

Missionaries
WEAR A
NAME TAG

ELDER WHITE

THE CHURCH OF
JESUS CHRIST
OF LATTER-DAY SAINTS

Missionaries wear a black name tag with our last name on it. A prophet has called us to represent the Lord Jesus Christ and His Church. We try to love people as the Savior did. It is an honor to wear His name over our hearts!

WHAT CAN YOU DO NOW?

Live as if the Savior were right beside you. Make good choices and let others see His light through you. Choose to love others as Christ loves us.

Missionaries TEACH

Missionaries teach people about the gospel. *Gospel* means "good news." The best news missionaries share is about Christ. Because of Him, we can live together with our families in the celestial kingdom forever.

WHAT CAN YOU DO NOW?

Offer to teach family home evenings. Be ready to participate in class discussions at church, and even be willing to teach part of the lesson.

Missionaries
WORK and SERVE

Missionaries work hard to spread the message of Jesus Christ. We try to give people hope for a better world. We show others this by giving service. Service means helping other people. We serve in many places such as senior citizen centers and homeless shelters.

WHAT CAN YOU DO NOW?

Work hard in school and at home. Choose to serve your family and friends without being asked. When you are old enough, consider getting a job in which you can interact with people. Happiness comes when you help others.

Missionaries share their testimonies everywhere and with everyone. A testimony is a belief in something that is true. When missionaries testify, we share with others how we feel about Jesus Christ and His gospel.

WHAT CAN YOU DO NOW?

Talk about the truths of the gospel with your family. Be bold in sharing your testimony when you have the opportunity. Heavenly Father will give you strength and confidence if you are willing to open your mouth.

Missionaries get REJECTED

Missionaries get told no all the time. Some people do not want to hear what we have to say. This is hard. But it helps us understand what Christ went through when He was on the earth. People rejected Him too. Like Christ, missionaries should still love those who say no.

WHAT CAN YOU DO NOW?

Disappointment is hard, but Jesus can help. Pray for strength when difficult times come. Talk with your parents about things you can do to feel better.

Missionaries BAPTIZE

Missionaries prepare those they teach for the saving ordinance of baptism. Baptism is for those who want to follow Jesus Christ. Once an elder baptizes someone, that person can receive the gift of the Holy Ghost. Then they become a member of The Church of Jesus Christ of Latter-day Saints.

WHAT CAN YOU DO NOW?

Prepare to be baptized when you are eight years old. Study this ordinance with your family. If you have already been baptized, review the covenants you made and remember how important it is to take the sacrament.

Missionaries have
the HOLY GHOST

The Holy Ghost helps missionaries to do everything on their missions. He helps us know where to go, what to do, whom to talk to, what to say, and how to love. Having the Spirit means being worthy. It does not mean we are perfect, but we are sincerely trying to be like Christ.

WHAT CAN YOU DO NOW?

Pray for the companionship of the Spirit and make choices that invite Him to be near you and help you. Try to recognize the Holy Ghost in your life. He is a voice you will feel more than hear.

Missionaries are
OBEDIENT

Missionaries obey a lot of rules. Those rules help keep us safe and guide us while serving. The Savior said, "If ye love me, keep my commandments."

WHAT CAN YOU DO NOW?

Choose to be obedient. Follow the rules in your home. Be willing to repent when you make mistakes. Repentance means to change and do better. You can find true happiness through obedience to Christ.

Missionaries EAT

Missionaries learn how to eat different kinds of food. Many meals are shared with Church members and families in the area. Most of the food is good, but some of it is gross! We enjoy eating with and meeting families.

WHAT CAN YOU DO NOW?

Help prepare meals for your family. Don't be afraid to try new foods—you might like it! Obey the Word of Wisdom.

Missionaries
are
CHRISTLIKE

Missionaries have faith, hope, and charity. We are kind, happy, and loving. Missionaries don't just act like Christ. We are trying to become more like Him.

WHAT CAN YOU DO NOW?

What we want and what we do make up who we are. *Preach My Gospel* chapter 6 can be a great tool in helping you become more like the Savior.

Missionaries INVITE all to come unto CHRIST

Missionaries want everyone to have the same happiness they do. We invite all people to accept the restored gospel. It is only through the grace and mercy of Jesus Christ that we can have peace and happiness in this life and for eternity.

WHAT CAN YOU DO NOW?

Many times the best testimony we share is how we act. To invite others to come unto Christ, we need to be like Him. When the time is right, share your testimony and invite others to come unto Christ.

"What do you think about missionaries now?"

"They're INCREDIBLE!"

"I want to be a missionary now so I'm ready to be a full-time missionary when I'm grown."

About the Author
BENJAMIN HYRUM WHITE

grew up in Northern California, where his love for reading was cultivated at an early age. Some of his favorite series are Dragonlance, Harry Potter, and the Beyonders. He served a full-time mission in the Rocky Mountains of Colorado. He met his wife, Keenan, in a clogging class at Brigham Young University while part of the International Folk Dance Ensemble. They now live in Utah Valley with their 4.5 kids. Ben enjoys going on dates with his wife and roughhousing with his kids. At BYU, he wrote "The History of *Preach My Gospel.*" His passion for missionary work continues with his other books: *10 Questions to Answer While Preparing for a Mission* and *10 Questions to Answer After Serving a Mission*.

About the Illustrator
COREY EGBERT

is a husband to an amazing wife, father to a super-cute little boy, and a humble subject to his cat, Rex. He can often be found taking pictures of run-down old buildings, obsessively reading books and blogs about art, and (secretly) watching documentaries about cheese. He loves illustrating and is still amazed that he gets to do it as a real job. He currently lives with his family in Virginia.